Sleep for Dessert

Sleep for Dessert

Olivia Elektra Willson-Piper

ISBN 978-989-33-4639-6

Illustrations by Soma Ishii
Front cover photo by Gerd Dibowski
Back cover photo by Siv Dibowski (Hanna, 1995)
Author photo by Anastasiia Zazuliak
All artwork used with permission

Edited and designed by Tell Tell Poetry

Printed in the United States of America

First Printing, 2023

Für meine Eltern

Contents

Acknowledgments

This book slowly materialised after a few years of hatching and dispatching, compiling and combining; and along the way, some marvellous people left their own ink splatters. I would like to celebrate those people:

Here's to my dad who, in his twenties, went places both inward and out; and to my mum who never stopped voyaging.

Here's to Marty who lives with childlike ardour.

Here's to Tell Tell Poetry for unveiling.

Here's to Soma for transforming.

Here's to Salah for visualising.

Here's to Gemma for vocalising.

Here's to Jed for investigating.

Here's to my friends for thickening water.

I would like to acknowledge that I will never become a fire dancer.

Sleep for Dessert

The Concept

Caravan Prelude

Bright night ballroom,
cavalcade coarse,
chrysalis costume,
spectacle force.

Firmament serenely staring—
charcoal eyes and sonorous blaring.
First position, crowd behold,
variations manifold.

The place, they landed just this morning—
the name, it skipped her mind.
Time keeps spinning without warning—
tomorrow's story's well-defined.

Service figure, fervid flicker.
Swirls and sweats, feather steps.
Dulcifying, limbs start flying,
scatter 'round the campus.

In a twist, her shape is shifting—
arms turn liquid, feet are lifting.
Radiant robotic roaring
gliding over people, pouring.

Enchanting blaze, alluring rays,
crimson waltz farewell.
Bodies tango, fly and split,
leaping into hell.

Nebulous inferno eating,
heating every single beating
heart that's gathered 'round,
silencing the motley ground.

The crowd explodes in cheer and lingers,
cherishing their fiery queen.
Bewitched by graceful sanguine fingers,
dancing en pointe in between.

Pirouettes of metal gliding,
spinning freely, balancing
silver stars that twirl and jangle,
filling pockets (save her own).

Her flames, they melt and drip and fade.
Turnout follows suit.
Content her clan is following
the carnival's pursuit.

Caravan Coda

Feathers on the Façade

A murmuration of starlings,
assembly of the neon people,
perfectly spaced—
feathers on the façade.

Chaffinch and chainsaw,
jackdaws and hammers,
common crane—
feathers on the façade.

Grids of gulls and sparrows,
dance of the sugarplum swallow
ruining the crisp concrete—
feathers on the façade.

Drills and trills,
nuts and fries,
primaveral levels—
feathers on the façade.

Octaves of chirps and chatter,
triple patterns,
a shaky sense of rhythm—
feathers on the façade.

Crowing at chromatic tits,
lovely like long locks underwater,
quality demolition—
feathers on the façade.

Little weekend stint to the coast.
First in Flight, flying kites,
from sandpaper to sandpiper—
feathers on the façade.

The Girl with the Oxytocin Perfume

Charlotta, with an "a"—
an electric echo of a vowel,
savoury and soft like bread dough
rising beneath chequered tea towels.

Her voice warped, her face blurred—
brown eyes, brown skin, brown hair.
Or did she have green eyes?
Age eclipsed the memory.

Zephyr carrying her scent
from the distant side of the classroom.
The girl with the oxytocin perfume
resides in higher echelons.

I trap my index
in the stapler.
The little goalposts
won't stand up straight.

If she wrote a snog—I mean a song—
I mean a piece—of her,
I would write the libretto,
stilettos bringing her up to my eyes.

I'm in a good place—
ylem near Big Bang,
sprinting down the escalator,
double-decker top front row.

We grab a coffee,
the machines are broken.
Sitting on blue velvet chairs,
I finger the studs.

And I disinvent the desire
when I catch her trilling hum,
her telling strum
at the sight of her man.

Curlicue Lashes

Kiss, kiss, kiss me through your curlicue lashes.
Black honey thickened on your cheeks,
which you keep purple.

Kiss, kiss, kiss me under the ceiling roots.
Show me all your stolid dance moves,
purr like nine o'clock.

Kiss, kiss, kiss me in your tesseract blanket tent.
Your orange lids squee silently
like children in socks.

Kiss, kiss, kiss me on that tiny, useless rocking horse.
Your canines going for a stroll—
attack and fall awake.

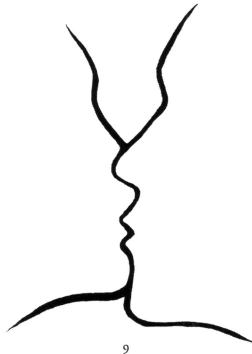

9

The Visitor

From the fever of the bath,
I see a dolphin in the tiles—
for sure, a shadow.

Was it there when I stabbed the surface?
Has it come to attend? With what intent?
Is it a friend?

Chummy creature—not a hippo, nor a poodle.
My puddle swells into a pond.
I squash a bomb.

My thalassic tub froths with forget-me-nots.
I dunk my head into the current,
spread the flow.

I'm drinking from the inlet.
Forty seconds,
then I leap.

I lean back,
enjoy the drought.
No more dolphin in the tiles.

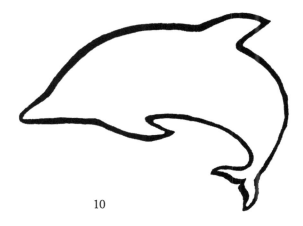

Torre de Água do Monte dos Congregados

Water towers tower
over and over,
white and un-wild
like ferrous jellyfish.

* * *

The Bubble

I alter my accent when I talk.
Received pronunciation swallows up all signs of me.
Nobody—NOBODY—can prick my map.

I alter my accent when I talk
to old men in poppy pyjamas,
patched up with afternoon television.

I drink black, red, and gold
from styrofoam straws,
sucking hard to loosen the block

                              -ck

                                   -ck

                                        -age.

I think of athletes, composers, poets, and painters,
philosophers, actors, scientists, and writers.
But I alter my accent when I talk.

Sugar

I prance into the kitchen,
hole in one sock.

The fridge door's light resistance
against my gentle pull

should be a hint—
six rows of European wealth.

Ringed fingers stretch.
The lump lies soft

and cold in my pregnant hand—
oily top, jaw workout.

Man-Hound

Sticky shine, an afternoon highlighted
like scholarly papers—
capable young oak.

Bipedal locomotion.
A stroll, then a meaty collision—
the Latin teacher with the thin wrists.

You catch a chat.
You haven't followed her fresh fellow.
Charming, I know.

Part of the pack,
she retrieves a tale—
hunt, pursuit,
deer stand purse.

A Picasso of a creature—
teeth like a slice of lime,
slime, cascading charisma.
You bite your lip.

She gushes over his appetite.
Positioned scratches.
An osmatic ordeal.

You're a cat's paw, not Napoleon's.
Yours is not vox populi.

Rats with Wings

Modena, Prague, Cologne, and Glasgow—
petrichor, the street lights Pernod,
prismatic arches, alameda,
trunks wet on one side in need of
lovebirds' carvings, hippie kisses.
Holding hands, his daughter listens
to eye-minded father's prudent musings:
Look, my girl, it's rats with wings.

Art Deco café, outdoor tables.
The waiters tall—half-Greek, half-angels.
Green tea, maybe a crêpe or two.
They start to hear a cashmere coo.
Girls in hijabs, boys eyeing boys,
a sudden hunch, a flutter noise.
Appalled, they add what bias brings:
Look around, it's rats with wings.

No viators, steadfast round,
elevated from the ground.
Their wings like sheets of slate, yet tough
like granite—brilliant, ashen, rough.
Random like a Dada poem.
Undulating, fear below them.
Once messengers of lords and kings—
Look, my dear, more rats with wings.

Plebeian, not a shred of doubt.
Alacrity to hate and shout.
Museum taxidermy peacock,
admiration for the nighthawk.
The fate of daisies long foregone,
yet red tulips linger on.
Everywhen it sits and sings,
they will cry: *It's rats with wings.*

Psychopath on a Cycle Path

On a halcyon day with nothing to do,
he cometh riding by—
the psychopath on a cycle path,
orbiting traffic bones.

With corybantic laughter
and picayune awareness,
imagining the slaughter
of all peasants.

Rhapsodic execution
as he's switching gears—
the psychopath on a cycle path,
orbiting traffic bones.

Equipped with orgulous grace
and a load of viridity,
ego á gogo—
Svengali of the pavement.

Upscale cladding,
insipience beneath—
the psychopath on a cycle path,
orbiting traffic bones.

God's Not Just Dead

BREAKING NEWS! BREAKING NEWS!
God's not just dead—
He's never been born.

The conception defused,
the wedding abed—
separate chamber returns.

God-Pa and God-Ma
were meeting at five—
he locked his keys in the car.

Cigarette postcards.
The booth near the stage.
Parmesan dip and two lattes.

All noughts and crosses,
quick, with the waiter.
Mistletoe bow and fake snow.

Stickman serviettes.
Toast illustrator.
Paying and leaving solo.

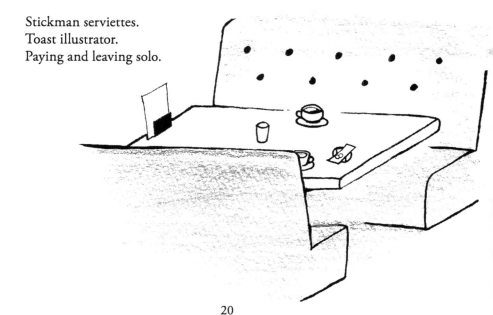

* * *

Modelling Dreams of a Mammoth

As the land tightens her onyx bonnet,
the village fragrance arrives
with singed bones.

Zigzag training grounds
of gossamer runways stretch along
ivory glaciers and waves of moss.

Clomp! like leaves in the breeze.
Float! with knotted arms.

Go-see behind a sweat curtain.
Surplus sunshine in the cracks.

Somersault sparks snuggle
as the midnight committee,
high on charcoal flour,
casts a hunting display.

The barrelled beast poses
with icicle tusks tucked and hairs split—

embosomed reflections of a dreadlocked
and maple-shaped anorak.

Obituary

I lost a friend today—
long-haired vintage woman.
I skimmed the local papers, as I often do,
searching for centenarians
and strangers' tragic accidents,
people born the same day,
sharing my name.
But there she was.

Her parents had picked a numinous phrase.
Something brief, along the lines of:
She's in a better place now.
She'd hate them for it.
The better place was an unadorned urn,
a domicile on someone's shelf,
her avenaceous ashes mixed with cardboard
and other people's bits.

She once told me she fancied a burial—
stargazing with rotten eyeballs in olive soil
with shoes on.
Preferable to the thought of being burnt—
your flesh shrivelled up,
teeth exposed,
roasted
like the corpses on *CSI*.

Some approached me and said:
At least she's not suffering anymore.
Except, no brain in Slumberland.
Expect to see her again one day.
Accept this is final.
They proceeded to apologise
when all I wanted to hear was:
FUCK!

Limb Photography

Imogen from Pepper Hill—
this story is about to kill
a sparkling daughter, twenty-one,
grand, sincere, forever gone.

Nurse Love, she cut the cord in two.
Father's face a squeamish blue.
Mother's sweaty forehead facing
the queen incarnate, hearts embracing.

Freebie magnets on the fridge.
Clarinet, near-perfect pitch.
Private school, double kiss,
dental metal, Latin wiz.

Ever-spinning record player.
Leather jacket, custom layer.
Music talk and lava lamps.
Looking forward to the dance.

April day, hidden rain.
Horseshoe tunnel, broken lane.
Velvet wind and velvet-eyed.
Dump your Vespa, hitch a ride.

Stunning seldom solitude.
Everybody loves the boots.
Wond'ring, *Will there be a bus?*
Yellow plates approaching fast.

* * *

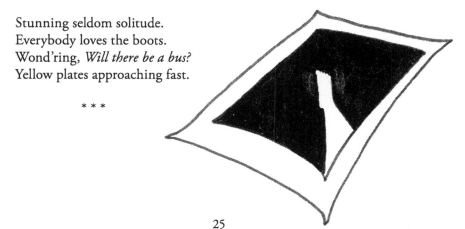

Imogen strapped to a bench—
cerebrum numb, uncommon stench.
Polaroids on the walls.
The creature wearing overalls.

The cabin cooked, the image raw.
Mr Newton grabs a saw.
Format, focus, flash, and flicker.
Exposure time, a busy clicker.

Mum and Dad on their own,
circling the landline phone.
Neighbours printing *Have You Seen Me?*
Imogen is on the TV.

Nestle in the cluster with the
garlic flowers, wee small hours.
A bed of rusty red, shape shattered,
teeny tiny pieces scattered.

German shepherds start to cry.
Law enforcement horrified.
Tolponds Road, the path is slippy.
Hair in her face, the perfect hippie.

Doorbell rings, they brought the priest.
Imogen was found deceased.
Timelapse, OBE.
Downfall of the bourgeoisie.

Careful colleagues dropping meals off,
trying to be extra soft.
Dad's newsboy cap rests on a stool.
No need to fill the garden pool.

Boardgame shelf collecting dust.
Someone take the dog, adjust.
Kitty sleeping in the closet.
Tins of untouched Easter chocolate.

After-Hours

In the cubicles,
the prayers begin at six o'clock,
when most of the figures left behind
wipe away their rubber marks
to leave for the pests
and the processions.

In the headquarters,
flying saucers drip from ceilings
like photonic polar bears
picking their liquid nitrogen paws.
Fixed above human heads,
they taste of migraine.

By the window,
chafing on woodchip wallpaper—
the year and dates. Apart from
the briefcase buzz and plate-shaped sweat,
alien accounts and plastic carnations,
striped foreheads and spectacle-shaped
nose tattoos—through the turnstiles,
faded espresso in a dress.

The clouds have broken.

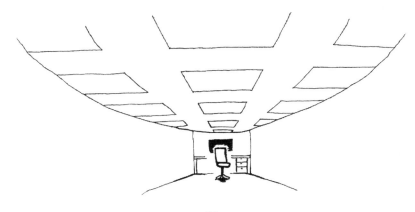

Manderley

Today I left Manderley.
It didn't go up in flames,
in fact, I'll re-enter
on occasion.

I no longer hear
the rattling of her chains
as she spooks
the insect room.

Like a basking shark
in Basking Shark Bay,
sucking it all in
for the flash.

She pissed on everything.
[Warning: Shock Hazard]
John Hancock puzzle—
had to use ink.

Resident charmer
jockeying for the crown.
Miss Moue,
still pulling buttons.

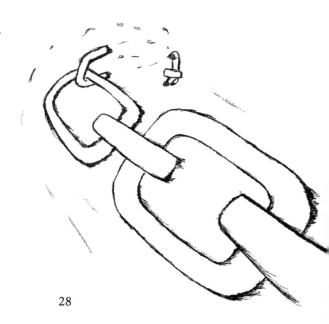

About the Author

Poet.   *Musician.*   *Explorer.*

To condense one's essence into so few words is a difficult feat, especially for Olivia Elektra Willson-Piper, who continues to unearth parts of herself through her ever-evolving poetry. A dual German-Swedish citizen with permanent residency in Portugal, she has experienced firsthand the magic of words and the stories they carry across continents and languages. As a linguaphile and passionate weaver of words, her aptitude for language transcends translation and dialect through her love of music. She's travelled the world as a violinist, exploring hidden corners and  catching glimpses of images that she holds in her mind until they pour out onto the page. Called to create in any way she can, Willson-Piper also shares her spoken poetry on YouTube, blending otherworldly visuals with lyrical verse to create an immersive storytelling experience.

Printed by Amazon Italia Logistica S.r.l.
Torrazza Piemonte (TO), Italy

51301131R00025